T0413266

Be An Expert!™

Ocean Animals

Amy Edgar

Children's Press®
An imprint of Scholastic Inc.

Contents

Know the Names

Be an expert! Get to know the names of these ocean animals.

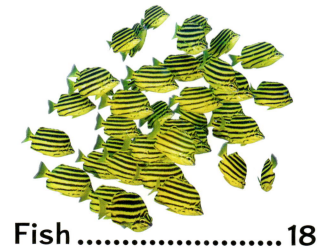

2

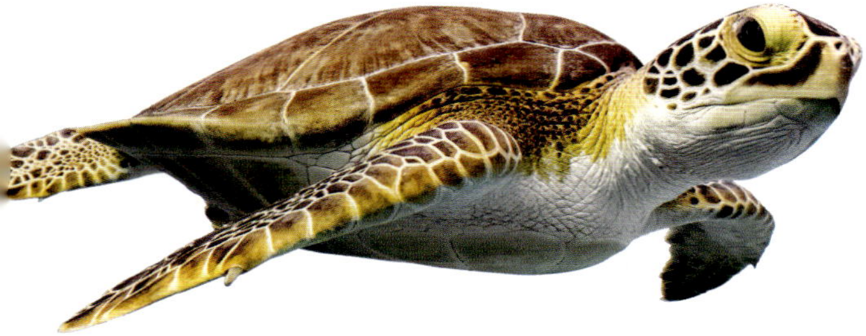

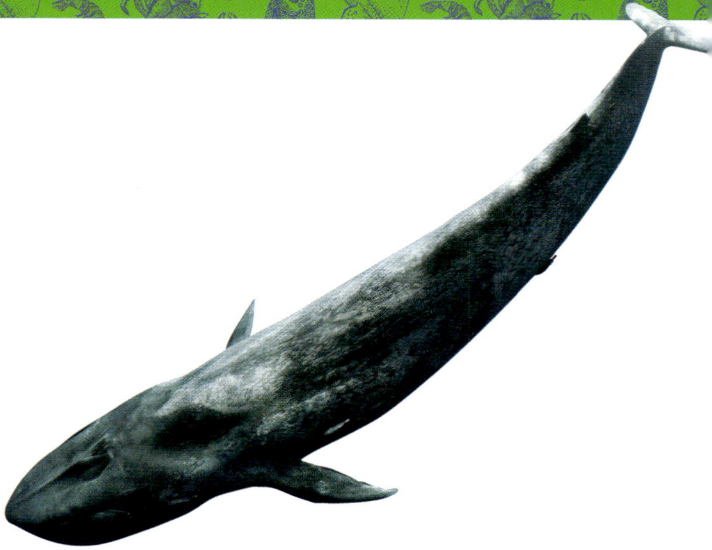

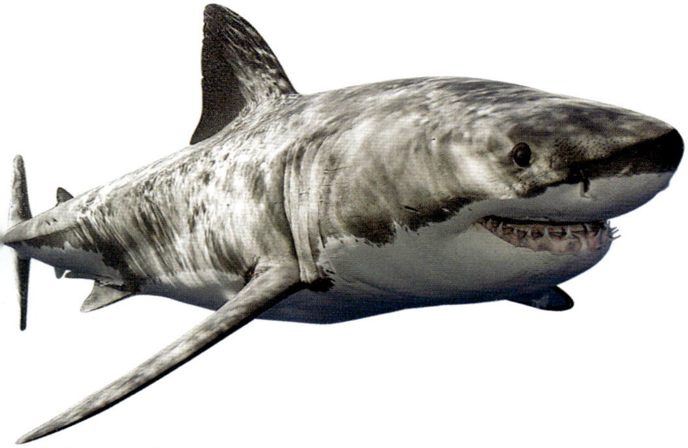

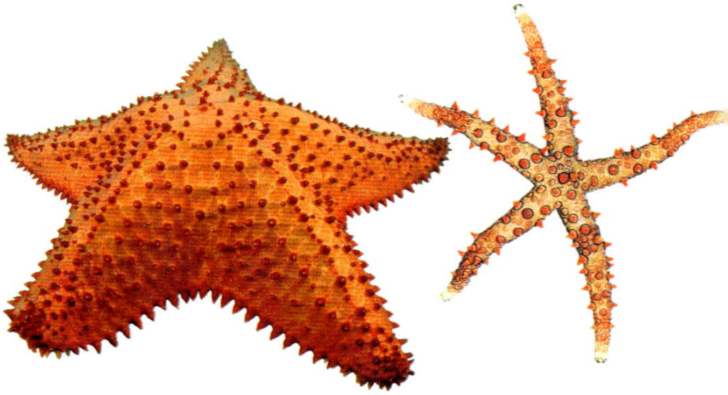

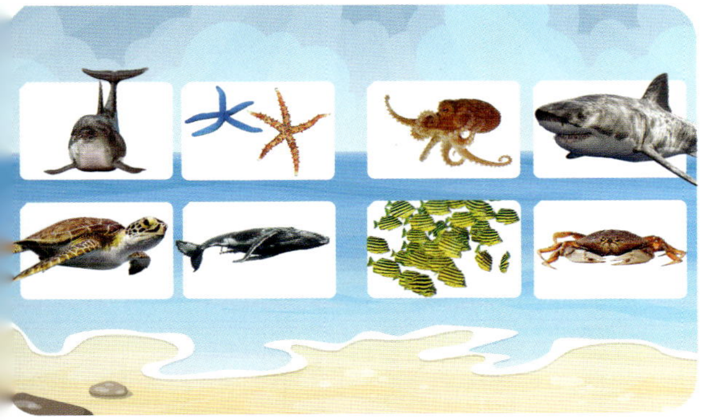

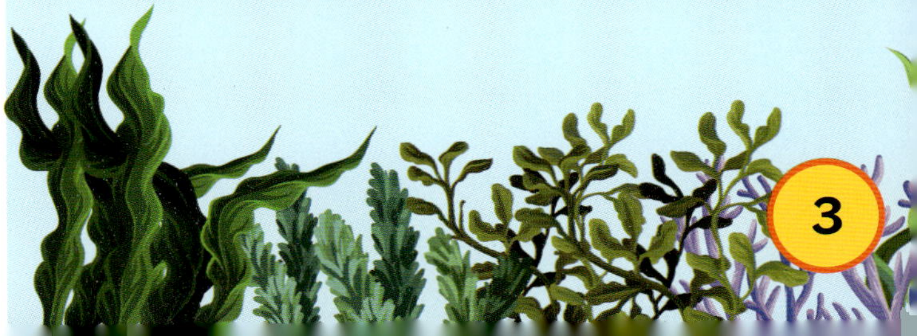

Dolphins

They are playful.
They **leap** and splash!

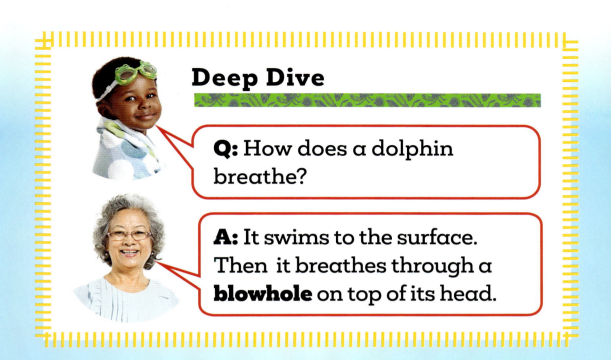

Deep Dive

Q: How does a dolphin breathe?

A: It swims to the surface. Then it breathes through a **blowhole** on top of its head.

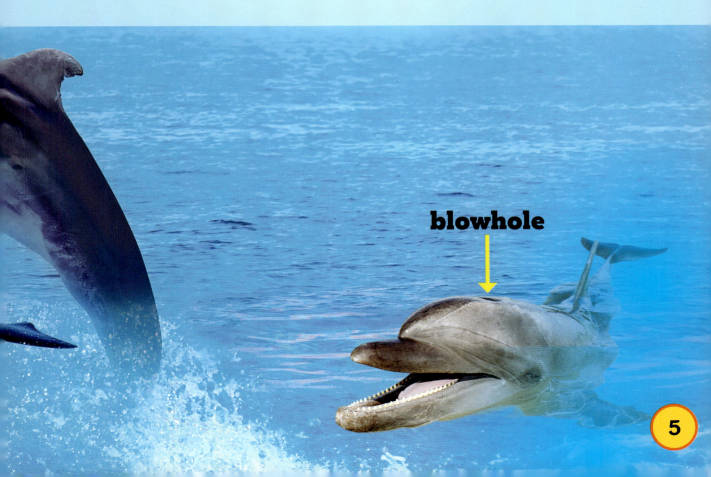

blowhole

Crabs

They have 10 legs.
Most walk sideways.

king crab

snow crabs

Expert Fact

Crabs shed their shells as they grow bigger. Then they grow new ones. This process is called molting.

blue crab

Dungeness crabs

Sea Turtles

They are great at swimming and diving. Their shells protect them.

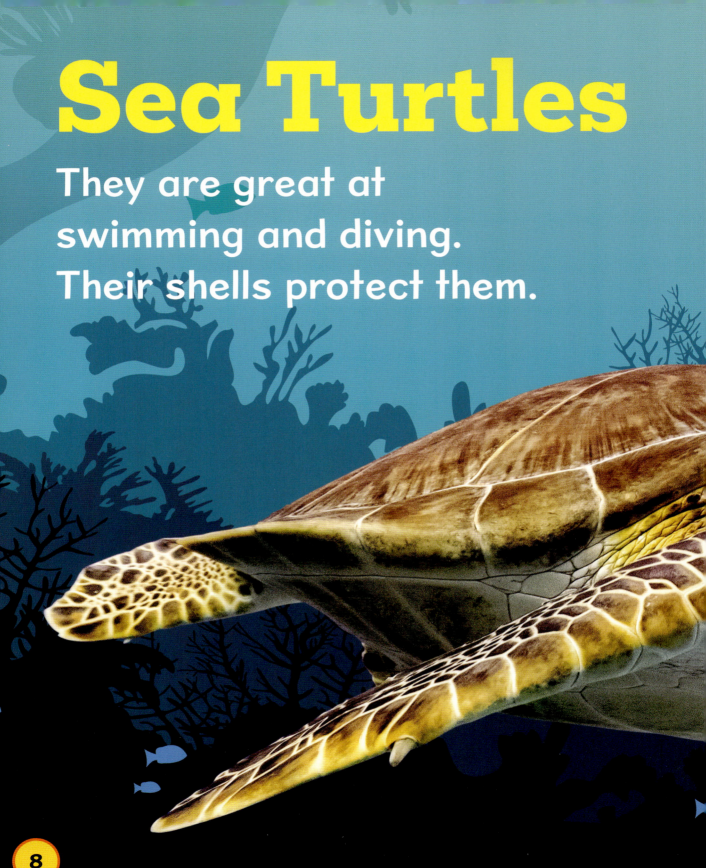

Zoom In

Find these parts in the big picture.

beak   **shell**   **claw**   **flippers**

Whales

They are the biggest animals on Earth. Some are almost as long as two school buses.

blue whale

Expert Fact

A whale's tail has two **flukes**. The flukes move up and down to push the whale through the water.

humpback whale

Octopuses

They have eight strong arms.

Deep Dive

Q: How do octopuses protect themselves from **predators**?

A: They change color or squirt ink.

Sharks

Chomp! Sharks have lots of teeth.

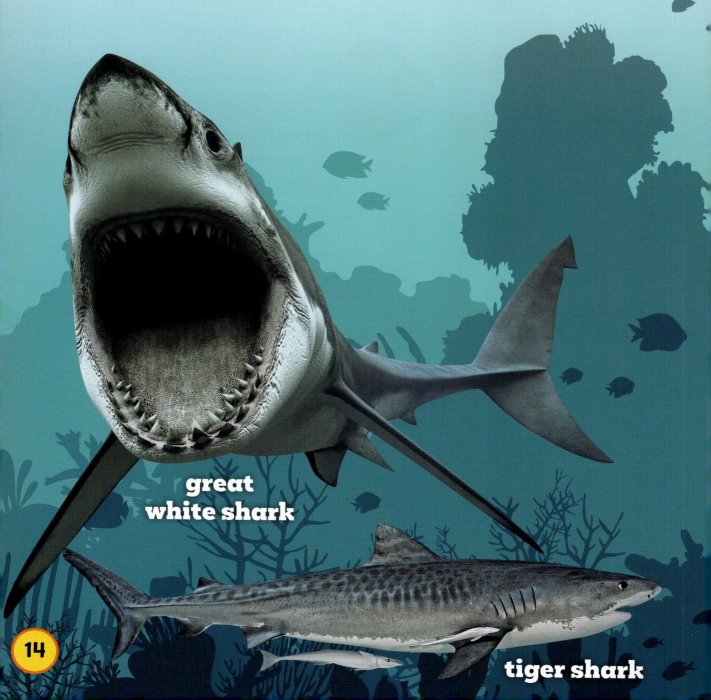

great white shark

tiger shark

14

Zoom In

Find these parts in the big picture.

| eye | pectoral fin | tail | gills |

saw shark

hammerhead sharks

Sea Stars

They have spiny arms.
If they lose an arm, they
grow a new one.

Deep Dive

Q: What do sea stars eat?

A: Sea stars eat clams and oysters. They have tiny suction cups under their arms. They use them to pry open the shells.

Fish

They breathe underwater.

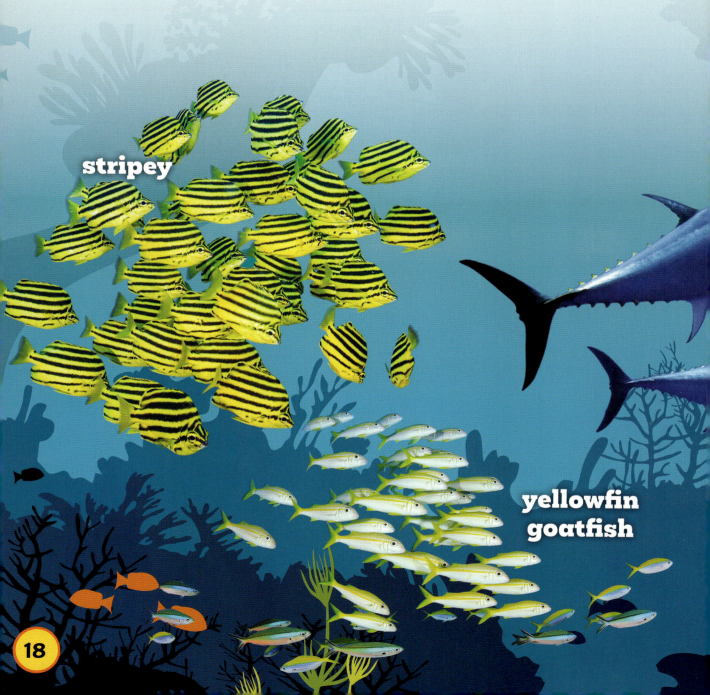

stripey

yellowfin
goatfish

cod

blue jack mackerel

tuna

Expert Fact

Most fish do not have eyelids. Their eyes are always open, even when they sleep.

All the Ocean Animals

They are amazing swimmers.
Thanks, ocean animals!

1.

2.

5.

6.

Expert Quiz

Do you know the names of these ocean animals? Then you are an expert! See if someone else can name them too!

3.

4.

7.

8.

Answers: 1. Dolphin. 2. Sea stars. 3. Octopus. 4. Shark. 5. Sea turtle. 6. Whale. 7. Fish. 8. Crab.

21

Expert Gear

Meet an ocean scientist, called an oceanographer. What does she need to study animals in the ocean?

She has an **oxygen tank**.

She has a **mask**.

She has **flippers**.

She has a **wet suit**.

Glossary

blowhole (BLOH-hohl): a nostril in the top of the head of a whale, dolphin, or porpoise, through which the animal can breathe.

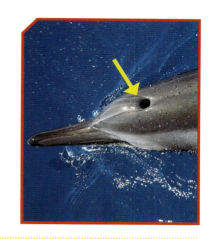

flukes (FLOOKS): parts of the tail of a sea creature such as a whale or dolphin.

leap (LEEP): to make a large jump.

predators (PRED-uh-turz): animals that live by hunting other animals for food.

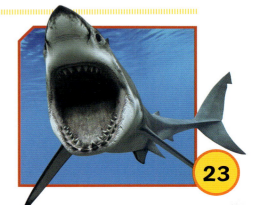

23

Index

Library of Congress Cataloging-in-Publication Data

Title: Ocean animals/by Amy Edgar.

Description: New York, NY: Children's Press, an imprint of Scholastic Inc., [2021] | Series: Be an expert! | Includes index. | Audience: Ages 4–5. | Audience: Grades K–1. | Summary: "Book introduces the reader to ocean animals"—Provided by publisher.

Identifiers: LCCN 2020031766 | ISBN 9780531136775 (library binding) | ISBN 9780531136782 (paperback)

Subjects: LCSH: Marine animals—Juvenile literature.

Classification: LCC QL122.2 .E34 2021 | DDC 591.77—dc23

LC record available at https://lccn.loc.gov/2020031766

Printed in Heshan, China 62

SCHOLASTIC, CHILDREN'S PRESS, BE AN EXPERT!™, and associated logos are trademarks and/or registered trademarks of Scholastic Inc.

1 2 3 4 5 6 7 8 9 10 R 30 29 28 27 26 25 24 23 22 21

Scholastic Inc., 557 Broadway, New York, NY 10012.

Art direction and design by THREE DOGS DESIGN LLC.

Photos ©: cover shark: by wildestanimal/Getty Images; cover top right sea star: sserg_dibrova/Getty Images; cover octopus: David Liittschwager/National Geographic Image Collection; cover bottom left sea star: Mathieu Foulquié/Biosphoto; back cover: Glenn Price/Dreamstime; 1 center left: Dmitry Miroshnikov/Getty Images; 1 crab: Glenn Price/Dreamstime; 2 top right: Sataporn Jiwjalaen/Dreamstime; 2 center right: David Liittschwager/National Geographic Image Collection; 2 bottom left: Rubberball/Mike Kemp/Getty Images; 2 bottom right: Gary Bell/Oceanwide/Minden Pictures; 3 top right: Alex Mustard/NPL/Minden Pictures; 3 center: Mathieu Foulquié/Biosphoto; 3 center right: sserg_dibrova/Getty Images; 5 sidebar top: Fuse/Getty Images; 5 bottom right: Norbert Probst/imageBROKER/Biosphoto; 6 top right: Sue Daly/Minden Pictures; 6 bottom: Jean-Pierre Sylvestre/Minden Pictures; 7 center: Sataporn Jiwjalaen/Dreamstime; 7 bottom: HQPhotos/Getty Images; 10–11 foreground: 90Alex Mustard/NPL/Minden Pictures; 11 sidebar bottom: Brandon Cole; 11 bottom: redbrickstock.com/Alamy Images; 13 sidebar top: FamVeld/Getty Images; 13 sidebar bottom: microdon/Getty Images; 14 bottom: SeaTops/imageBROKER/Biosphoto; 15 left: Saul Gonor/Blue Planet Archive; 15 right: Dmitry Miroshnikov/Getty Images; 15 sidebar right: SeaTops/imageBROKER/Biosphoto; 16-17 sea star: Mathieu Foulquié/Biosphoto; 16 top: sserg_dibrova/Getty Images; 16 center left: Dominique Delfino/Biosphoto; 17 sidebar top: Fuse/Getty Images; 18 top left: Gary Bell/Oceanwide/Minden Pictures; 19 right: Franco Banfi/Biosphoto/Minden Pictures; 20 top right: sserg_dibrova/Getty Images; 20 bottom right: redbrickstock.com/Alamy Images; 21 sidebar: Rubberball/Mike Kemp/Getty Images; 21 bottom left: Gary Bell/Oceanwide/Minden Pictures; 21 bottom right: Glenn Price/Dreamstime; 22 center: Andy Mann/National Geographic Image Collection; 23 center top: Wildlife GmbH/Alamy Images; 23 center bottom: Lisa Tichane/Offset.

All other photos © Shutterstock.